The Seven Continents

Asia

by A. R. Schaefer

Consultant:
Mark Healy
Professor of Geography
William Rainey Harper College
Palatine, Illinois

Capstone
press

Mankato, Minnesota

Bridgestone Books are published by Capstone Press,
151 Good Counsel Drive, P.O. Box 669, Mankato, Minnesota 56002.
www.capstonepress.com

Library of Congress Cataloging-in-Publication Data
Schaefer, A. R. (Adam Richard), 1976–
    Asia / A. R. Schaefer.
    p. cm.—(Bridgestone books. The seven continents)
    Summary: "Describes the continent of Asia, including climate, landforms, plants, animals,
countries, people, as well as Asia and the world"—Provided by publisher.
    Includes bibliographical references and index.
    ISBN-13: 978-0-7368-5427-6 (hardcover)
    ISBN-10: 0-7368-5427-4 (hardcover)
    1. Asia—Juvenile literature. 2. Asia—Geography—Juvenile literature. I. Title. II. Series: Seven
continents (Mankato, Minn.)
DS5.S33 2006
950—dc22
                            2005018054

Editorial Credits

Becky Viaene, editor; Patrick D. Dentinger, designer; Kim Brown and Tami Collins, map illustrators;
    Wanda Winch, photo researcher; Scott Thoms, photo editor

Photo Credits

Corbis/Craig Lovell, 10 (middle); Corbis/David Ball, 1; Corbis/Dean Conger, cover (foreground);
Corbis/Gavriel Jecan, 6 (left); Corbis/George Steinmetz, 6 (bottom right); Corbis/Macduff Everton,
10 (bottom); Corbis/Robert Holmes, 18 (bottom); Corbis/Setboun, 6 (top right); Corbis/Tiziana
and Gianni Baldizzone, 10 (top); Corel, 20; Digital Vision/Gerry Ellis, 12 (bottom right); Digital
Vision/Gerry Ellis and Karl Ammann, 12 (left); Doranne Jacobson, 18 (top); Map Resources, cover
(background), Peter Arnold Inc./Lynn Rogers, 12 (top right); Peter Arnold Inc./Shehzad Noorani, 16

1 2 3 4 5 6 11 10 09 08 07 06

Table of Contents

Continents of the World

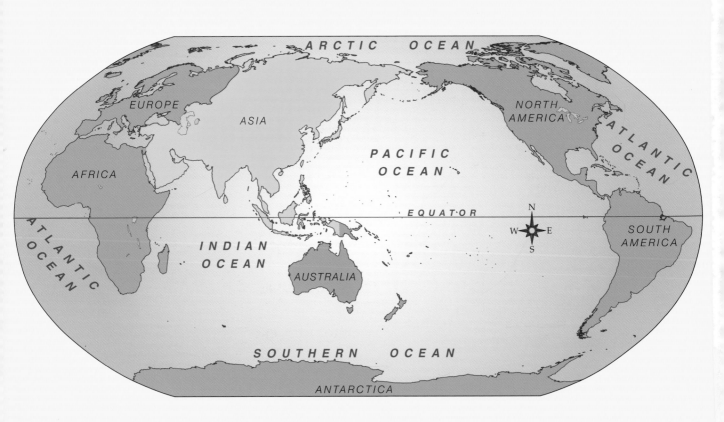

Asia

Asia is the biggest landmass in the world. It stretches across more than 17 million square miles (44 million square kilometers).

With three-fifths of the world's people, Asia also has the largest population of any continent. Bicyclists zip through crowded streets. Farmers grow rice in the country. **Nomads** cross a dusty **desert**. Siberians hike on snow-covered mountains. Across this giant continent, Asia's people are as varied as the land.

◄ Asia connects to Europe and Africa. This continent takes up almost one-third of the earth's land.

Climate

Climate across Asia ranges from the cold, icy north to the hot, rainy south. Northern areas are covered with snow year-round. Moving south, Asia has four distinct seasons. Central Asia includes cold mountain climates and hot desert climates. Deserts also cover large areas of southwestern Asia.

Unlike the dry southwest, southeast Asia has long periods of wet weather. Strong seasonal winds, called **monsoons**, bring heavy rainfall to Asia's **rain forests**.

◀ Rain forests, snow-covered mountains, and sandy deserts cover Asia's land.

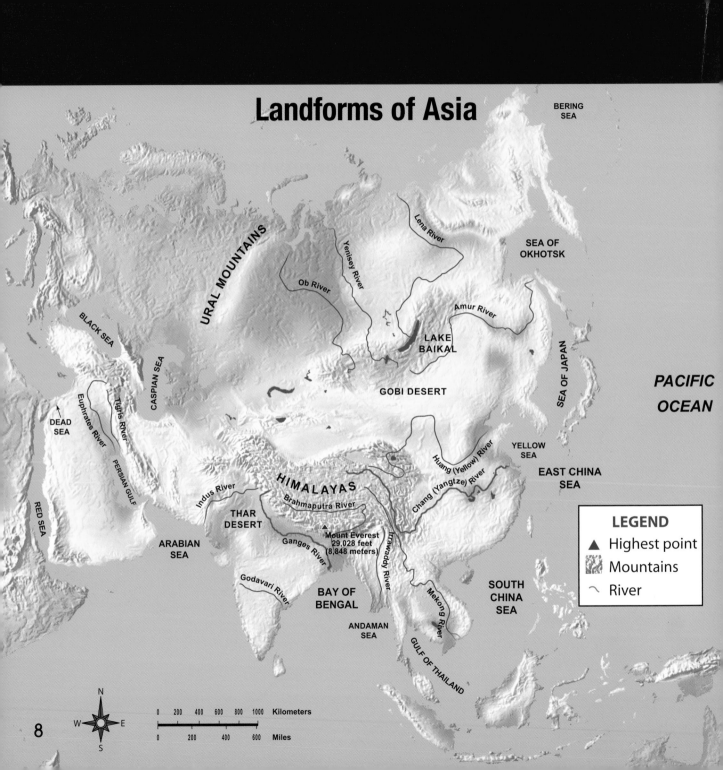

Landforms of Asia

BERING SEA

URAL MOUNTAINS

Lena River

Yenisey River

Ob River

SEA OF OKHOTSK

Amur River

LAKE BAIKAL

GOBI DESERT

SEA OF JAPAN

PACIFIC OCEAN

BLACK SEA

CASPIAN SEA

DEAD SEA

Euphrates River

Tigris River

PERSIAN GULF

RED SEA

Huang (Yellow) River

YELLOW SEA

EAST CHINA SEA

Chang (Yangtze) River

HIMALAYAS

Indus River

Brahmaputra River

THAR DESERT

ARABIAN SEA

Ganges River

Mount Everest
29,028 feet
(8,848 meters)

Irrawaddy River

Godavari River

BAY OF BENGAL

Mekong River

SOUTH CHINA SEA

ANDAMAN SEA

GULF OF THAILAND

LEGEND
▲ Highest point
░ Mountains
∿ River

8

N
W E
S

| 0 | 200 | 400 | 600 | 800 | 1000 | Kilometers |

| 0 | 200 | 400 | 600 | Miles |

Landforms

In Asia, people can climb to the world's highest point and swim in the lowest. Part of the Himalayas, Mount Everest is the world's tallest mountain. It is 29,028 feet (8,848 meters) tall. West of the Himalayas, people swim in the salty Dead Sea. It drops 1,312 feet (400 meters) below sea level.

Asians depend on the continent's rivers and lakes. The Chang and Ganges rivers are used to water crops. The world's largest lake, the Caspian Sea, provides fish and oil.

Plants

Thousands of different plants grow in Asia's many climates. Besides moss, few plants grow in Asia's cold north. In warmer areas to the south, forests of fir and pine grow. Colorful wildflowers and tall grasses cover central Asia's dry land.

Plants that are grown in the warm, wet climate of south and east Asia are sold worldwide. Much of the world's tea, rubber, and bamboo grow there. Farmers also grow rice, wheat, and cotton in these areas.

◀ Evergreen forests, colorful wildflowers, and rice fields grow in Asia's varied climates.

Animals

Thick fur keeps Arctic foxes and reindeer warm in cold northern Asia. Farther south, snow leopards move quietly across the mountains to catch sheep and goats.

Asia's hot, southern rain forests are full of animals. Playful red orangutans swing from tall trees. On the ground below, Asian elephants munch on plants.

Today, Asia is the only place where certain kinds of **endangered** animals live in the wild. Pandas and tigers make their homes in Asia's shrinking wilderness.

◄ Endangered animals, including orangutans, snow leopards, and giant pandas, live in Asia.

Countries of Asia

ARCTIC OCEAN

RUSSIA

RUSSIA (EUROPE)

EUROPE

KAZAKHSTAN

MONGOLIA

AZERBAIJAN

KYRGYZSTAN

GEORGIA

TAJIKISTAN

ARMENIA

UZBEKISTAN

TURKEY

TURKMENISTAN

CYPRUS

SYRIA

IRAN

AFGHANISTAN

LEBANON

IRAQ

BAHRAIN

ISRAEL

QATAR

PAKISTAN

JORDAN

KUWAIT

SAUDI ARABIA

UNITED ARAB EMIRATES

OMAN

YEMEN

CHINA

BHUTAN

NEPAL

INDIA

MYANMAR

BANGLADESH

THAILAND

NORTH KOREA

JAPAN

SOUTH KOREA

PACIFIC OCEAN

TAIWAN

LAOS

VIETNAM

CAMBODIA

PHILIPPINES

BRUNEI

MALAYSIA

MALDIVES

SRI LANKA

AFRICA

SINGAPORE

INDONESIA

PAPUA NEW GUINEA

EAST TIMOR

Kilometers
0   500   1000
0   620
Miles

INDIA OCEAN

INDIAN OCEAN

AUSTRALIA

14

Countries

About 3.9 billion people live in Asia's 49 countries. Russia is the largest in size. Russia is so big that part of it is in Europe.

China and India have large populations. More than 1 billion people live in each country. But China is the world's most populated country, with 1.2 billion people.

Asia also has some of the world's biggest cities. Mumbai, India, is home to more than 12 million people. About 34 million people live in and around Tokyo, Japan.

Population Density of Asia

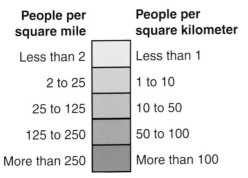

People per square mile		People per square kilometer
Less than 2		Less than 1
2 to 25		1 to 10
25 to 125		10 to 50
125 to 250		50 to 100
More than 250		More than 100

• Major Cities/Urban Centers
More than 7.5 million people

People

Hundreds of religions and languages can be found in Asia. Of Asia's many religions, Hinduism has the largest number of followers. Many Asians also practice Islam or Buddhism.

Of Asia's languages, Chinese has the most speakers with more than 1 billion. Millions of Asians speak Japanese and Korean. Many Asians also speak Russian or Arabic.

◄ Outside of Asian cities, children attend school in simple wooden buildings.

Living in Asia

In Asia, city life is very different from country life. In large crowded cities, many people live in apartment buildings. They have many choices of food and clothing. Most people wear **modern** clothing.

Outside of Asia's cities, people live in small wood or mud homes. Country life leaves people with few food or clothing choices. Most people eat rice and vegetables that they grow. People often make their own clothing, including **traditional** outfits.

◄ In Gujarat, India, people live in baked earth homes. In Tokyo, Japan, people live in modern apartments.

Asia and the World

Asia is called the cradle of **civilization**. Asians were the first to farm, make laws, and create cities. The first paper and writing system also began in Asia.

Asian **culture**, especially its religions, has also influenced the world. All of the world's main religions, including Buddhism, Christianity, Hinduism, Judaism, and Islam, began on this continent. There's no doubt that this continent has made a huge impact on the world.

◀ A holy site to Jews, the Western Wall, and a holy site to Muslims, Dome of the Rock, are in Jerusalem, Israel.

Glossary

civilization (siv-i-luh-ZAY-shuhn)—an advanced stage of human organization, technology, and culture

culture (KUHL-chur)—a people's way of life, ideas, art, customs, and traditions

desert (DEZ-urt)—a very dry area of land; deserts receive less than 10 inches (25 centimeters) of rain each year.

endangered (en-DAYN-jurd)—at risk of dying out

modern (MOD-urn)—up-to-date or new in style

monsoon (mon-SOON)—a very strong seasonal wind that brings heavy rains or hot, dry weather

nomad (NOH-mad)—a person who moves from place to place to find food and water

rain forest (RAYN FOR-ist)—a tropical forest where much rain falls

traditional (truh-DISH-uhn-uhl)—having styles, manners, and ways of the past

Read More

Sayre, April Pulley. *Greetings, Asia!* Our Amazing Continents. Brookfield, Conn.: Millbrook Press, 2003.

Vierow, Wendy. *Asia.* Atlas of the Seven Continents. New York: PowerKids Press, 2004.

Internet Sites

FactHound offers a safe, fun way to find Internet sites related to this book. All of the sites on FactHound have been researched by our staff. Here's how:

1. Visit *www.facthound.com*

2. Type in this special code **0736854274** for age-appropriate sites. Or enter a search word related to this book for a more general search.

3. Click on the **Fetch It** button.

FactHound will fetch the best sites for you!

Index